Fig. 2. General view of part of the Library attached to the Church of S. Wallberg at Zutphen. Frontispiece

Libraries in the Medieval and Renaissance Periods

*THE REDE LECTURE,
DELIVERED JUNE 13, 1894*

By

John Willis Clark M.A., F.S.A.

REGISTRARY OF THE UNIVERSITY, AND
FORMERLY FELLOW OF TRINITY COLLEGE,
CAMBRIDGE.

The lecture was illustrated by lantern-slides. A brief notice of each of these is printed in the text in Italics at the place in the lecture where the slide was exhibited.

Cover Photograph: SantiMB

ISBN: 978-1-78139-035-1

© 2011 Benediction Classics, Oxford.

Illustrations

Fig. 2. General view of part of the Library attached to the Church of S. Wallberg at Zutphen. Frontispiece 2
Fig. 1. Interior of a library: from a MS. of a French translation of the first book of the Consolations of Philosophy of Boethius. 16
Fig. 3. Desk in the library at Zutphen: from a photograph. 17
Fig. 4. Bookcase in Hereford Cathedral. (Lent by the Syndics of the University Press.) 19
Fig. 5. Bookcases in the library of the University of Leiden: from a print by J.C. Woudanus, dated 1610. (Lent by the Syndics of the University Press.) 21
Fig. 6. Bookcases at west end of south side of Library, Cesena. 22
Fig. 7. Part of a single bookcase in the Library, Cesena. 23

List of Lantern Slides

Bookcase in the Codex Amiatinus: from Garrucci, "Storia dell' arte Cristiana," iii. pl. 126. 3
Interior of part of the Vatican Library. 4
Part of the north walk of the cloister, Durham. 8
Cupboard from sacristy of Bayeux Cathedral. 9
Book-recess, east walk of the cloister, Worcester. 9
Views of S. Germain des Prés: (1) from Franklin, "Anciennes Bibliothèques de Paris," i. 126; (2) from Bouillart, "Histoire de l'Abbaye de S. Germain des Préz." 11
View of Citeaux: from Viollet-Le-Duc, "Dictionnaire de l'Architecture," i. 271. 12
Library of Christ's Hospital: from Trollope's "History of Christ's Hospital," p. 105. 13
Merton College, Oxford: (1) general view of the interior of the Library; (2) a single bookcase as at present. 19
Bookcase in the Library of Corpus Christi College, Oxford. 20
Bookcase in the Library of Trinity Hall, Cambridge. 20
Bookcase in the Medicean Library at Florence. 24
Bookcases in S. John's College Library. 24
Bookcase in Peterhouse Library. 24
Interior of the Library of the Escurial and of the Bibliothèque Mazarine, Paris. 25
One compartment of Trinity College Library. 26
Book-cupboard and desk at Bolton, Lancashire. The former is lettered: "The gift of Mr James Leaver, citison of London 1694." 26

LIBRARIES.

A library may be considered from two very different points of view: as a workshop, or as a Museum.

The former commends itself to the practical turn of mind characteristic of the present day; common sense urges that mechanical ingenuity, which has done so much in other directions, should be employed in making the acquisition of knowledge less cumbrous and less tedious; that as we travel by steam, so we should also read by steam, and be helped in our studies by the varied resources of modern invention. There lies on my table at this present moment a *Handbook of Library Appliances*, in which fifty-three closely printed pages are devoted to this interesting subject, with illustrations of various contrivances by which the working of a large library is to be facilitated and brought up to date. In fact, from this point of view a library may be described as a gigantic mincing-machine, into which the labours of the past are flung, to be turned out again in a slightly altered form as the literature of the present.

If, on the other hand, a library be regarded as a Museum—and I use the word in its original sense as a temple or haunt of the Muses—very different ideas are evoked. Such a place is as useful as the other—every facility for study is given—but what I may call the personal element as affecting the treasures there assembled is brought prominently forward. The development of printing, as the result of individual effort; the art of bookbinding, as practised by different persons in different countries; the history of the books themselves, the libraries in which they have found a home, the hands that have turned their pages, are there taken note of. Modern literature is fully represented, but the men of past

Libraries in the Medieval and Renaissance Periods

days are not thrust out of sight; their footsteps seem to linger in the rooms where once they walked—their shades seem to protect the books they once handled. What Browning felt about frescoes may be applied—*mutatis mutandis*—to books in such an asylum as I am trying to portray:

> *Wherever a fresco peels and drops,*
> *Wherever an outline weakens and wanes*
> *Till the latest life in the painting stops,*
> *Stands One whom each fainter pulse-tick pains:*
> *One, wishful each scrap should clutch the brick,*
> *Each tinge not wholly escape the plaster,*
> *A lion who dies of an ass's kick,*
> *The wronged great soul of an ancient Master.*

ROMAN It may be safely asserted that at no time has a love of reading, a desire to be fairly well-informed on all sorts of subjects, been so widely diffused as at the present day. As a necessary consequence of this the 'workshop' view of a library has been very generally accepted. I have no wish to undervalue it; I only plead for the recognition of another sentiment which may at times be overlaid by the pressure of daily avocations. In Cambridge, at least, there is no fear that it should ever be obliterated altogether, for we have effected a happy alliance between the present and the past, by which neither is neglected, neither is unduly prominent. This being the case, it has occurred to me that I may be so fortunate as to interest a Cambridge audience while I set before them some of the results at which I have arrived in investigating the position, the arrangement, and the fittings of libraries in the medieval and renaissance periods. It will, of course, be impossible to attempt more than a sketch of so extensive a subject, and I fear that I must omit the contents of the bookcases altogether; but I shall hope, by a selection of typical illustrations, to make you realise what some of the libraries, monastic, public, or private, that fall within my period were like.

LIBRARIES. I must begin with a few words about Roman libraries, because their methods influenced the Middle Ages, and are, in fact, the precursors of those in fashion in our own times. The Romans preserved their books in two ways: either in a small room or closet, for reading elsewhere; or in a large apartment, fitted up with greater or less splendour, according to the taste or the means of the possessor, in which the books were doubtless studied as in a modern library. An instructive example of the former class was one of the first discoveries at Herculaneum in 1754. It was a very small room, so small in fact that a man who stood with his arms extended in the centre of it could almost touch the walls on either side, yet 1700 rolls were found in it. These were kept in wooden presses (*armaria*) which stood against the walls like a modern bookcase. Besides these a rectangular case occupied the central space, with only a narrow passage to the right and left between it and the wall-cases. These cases were about a man's height, and had been numbered. It may be concluded from this that a catalogue of the books had once existed. In larger libraries the books were kept in similar presses, but they were ornamented with the busts or pictures of illustrious men, under each of which was a suitable inscription, usually in verse.

No ancient figure of one of these book-presses has been preserved, so far as I have been able to ascertain; but, as furniture is apt to retain its original forms with but little variation for a very long period, a representation of a press containing the four Gospels, which occurs among the mosaics in the Mausoleum of the Empress Galla Placidia at Ravenna, though it could not have been executed before the middle of the fifth century, may be taken as a fairly accurate picture of the book-presses of an earlier age. It is unnecessary to describe it, for it is exactly like a still later example which I am about to shew you. This picture occurs at the beginning of the MS. of the Vulgate called the *Codex Amiatinus*, which is now proved to have been written in England, at Wearmouth or Jarrow, but probably by an Italian scribe, shortly before 716. The seated figure represents Ezra writing the Law.

Bookcase in the Codex Amiatinus: from Garrucci, "Storia dell' arte Cristiana," iii. pl. 126.

To get an idea of one of the larger Roman libraries in ancient times we cannot do better than turn to that of the Vatican at the present day. It was fitted up as we see it now—with presses, busts, and antique vases, by Pope Sixtus V., in 1588. It is therefore, at best, only a modern antique; but arranged so skilfully that an ancient Roman, if he could come to life again, might imagine himself in his own library.

Libraries in the Medieval and Renaissance Periods

Interior of part of the Vatican Library.

RULE OF S. BENEDICT. The library-era, as we may call it, of the Christian world, began with the publication of the Rule of S. Benedict, early in the sixth century. But, just as that Rule emphasized and arranged on the lines of an ordered system observances which had long been practised by isolated congregations or individuals living in solitude—so the part of it which deals with study was evidently no new thing. S. Benedict did not invent literature or libraries; he only lent the sanction of his name to the study of the one and the formation of the other. That libraries existed before his period is proved by allusions to them in the Fathers and other early writers; but, as those allusions are general, and say nothing from which either their size or their arrangement can be inferred, I shall dismiss them in very few sentences. The earliest is said to have been the collection got together at Jerusalem, by Bishop Alexander, at the beginning of the third century. Another was founded about fifty years later at Cæsarea by Origen. This is described as not only extensive, but remarkable for the importance of the manuscripts it contained. Others are recorded at Hippo, at Cirta, at Constantinople, and at Rome, where both S. Peter's and the Lateran had their special collections of books. I suspect that all these libraries were in connexion with churches, possibly actually within their walls. At Cirta, for example, it is recorded that during the persecution of 303-304 the officers "went to the church where the Christians used to assemble, and spoiled it of chalices, lamps, etc., but when they came into the library (*bibliothecam*), the presses (*armaria*) there were found empty." This language seems to imply that the sacred vessels and the books were in different parts of the same building. The instructions, again, of the dying Augustine, who bequeathed his library to the church at Hippo, lead to the same conclusion. The library of S. Peter's at Rome, though added to the basilica erected by Constantine, long after its primitive foundation, was on the ground-floor in the angle between the nave and the north limb of the transept, a position which may perhaps have been selected in accordance with early usage.

LIBRARIES IN CHURCHES. I now pass to the treatment of books in the libraries of the monastic orders. These either adopted the Rule of S. Benedict, or based their own Rule upon its provisions. It will therefore be desirable to examine what he said on the subject of study, and I will translate a few lines from the 48th chapter of his Rule, *Of daily manual labour.*

RULE OF S. BENEDICT.

Idleness is the enemy of the soul; hence brethren ought, at certain seasons, to occupy themselves with manual labour, and again, at certain hours, with holy reading....

Between Easter and the calends of October let them apply themselves to reading from the fourth hour till near the sixth hour. After the sixth hour, when they rise from table, let them rest on their beds in complete silence; or, if any one should wish to read to himself, let him do so in such a way as not to disturb any one else....

HIS INFLUENCE.

From the calends of October to the beginning of Lent let them apply themselves to reading until the second hour.... During Lent, let them apply themselves to reading from morning until the end of the third hour ... and, in these days of Lent, let them receive a book apiece from the library, and read it straight through. These books are to be given out at the beginning of Lent. It is important that one or two seniors should be appointed to go round the monastery at the hours when brethren are engaged in reading, in case some ill-conditioned brother should be giving himself up to sloth or idle talk, instead of reading steadily; so that not only is he useless to himself, but incites others to do wrong.

"Behold! how great a matter a little fire kindleth!" These simple words, uttered by one who in power of far-reaching influence has had no equal, gave an impulse to study in the ages it once was the fashion to call dark which grew with the growth of the Order—till wherever a Benedictine house arose—or a monastery of any one of the Orders which were but off-shoots from the Benedictine tree—books were multiplied, and a library came into being, small indeed at first, but increasing year by year, till the wealthier houses had gathered together a collection of books that would do credit to a modern University.

Libraries in the Medieval and Renaissance Periods

MONASTIC CUSTOMS. It is very interesting to notice, as Order after Order was founded, a steady development of feeling with regard to books, and an ever increasing care for their safe-keeping. S. Benedict had contented himself with general directions for study; the Cluniacs prescribe the selection of a special officer to take charge of the books, with an annual audit of them, and the assignment of a single volume to each brother; the Carthusians and the Cistercians provide for the loan of books to extraneous persons under certain conditions—a provision which the Benedictines in their turn adopted. Further, by the time that the Cluniac Customs were drawn up in the form in which they have come down to us, it is evident that the number of books exceeded the number of brethren; for both in them, and in the statutes which Lanfranc promulgated for the use of the English Benedictines in 1070, the keeper of the books is directed to bring all the books of the House into Chapter, after which the brethren, one by one, are to bring in the books they had borrowed on the same day in the previous year. Some of the former class of books were probably service-books, but, after this deduction has been made, we may fairly conclude that by the end of the eleventh century Benedictine Houses possessed two sets of books: (1) those which were distributed among the brethren; (2) those which were kept in some safe place, probably the church, as part of the valuables of the House: or, to adopt modern phrases, they had a lending library and a library of reference. The Augustinians go a step farther than the Benedictines and the Orders derived from them, for they prescribe the kind of press in which the books are to be kept. Both they and the Premonstratensians permit their books to be lent on the receipt of a pledge of sufficient value. Lastly, the Friars, though they were established on the principle of holding no possessions of any kind, soon found that books were indispensable; that, in the words of a Norman Bishop, *Claustrum sine armario, castrum sine armamentario.* So, by a strange irony, it came to pass that their libraries excelled those of most other Orders, as Richard de Bury testifies in the *Philobiblon*.

DISTRIBUTION OF BOOKS.

THE MENDICANT ORDERS.

Whenever we turned aside to the cities and places where the Mendicants had their convents ... we found heaped up amidst the utmost poverty the utmost riches of wisdom....

These men are as ants ever preparing their meat in the summer, and ingenious bees continually fabricating cells of honey.... And to pay due regard to truth, although they lately at the eleventh hour have entered the Lord's vineyard ..., they have added more in this brief hour to the stock of the sacred books than all the other vine-dressers; following in the footsteps of Paul, the last to be called but the first in preaching, who spread the gospel of Christ more widely than all others.

USE OF THE CLOISTER. It might have been expected, from the use of the word *library* in the Rule of S. Benedict, that a special room assigned to books would have been one of the primitive component parts of every Benedictine House. This, however, is not the case. Such a room does usually occur in these Houses, but it will be found, on examination, that it was added to some previously existing structure in the fourteenth or fifteenth century. Its absence from the primitive plan brings out two points very clearly: (1) how few books even a wealthy community could afford to possess for several centuries after the foundation of the Order; (2) how strictly the Order adhered to prescribed arrangements in laying out its Houses, for even those built, or rebuilt, after books had become plentiful, do not admit a Library as an indispensable item in their ground-plan.

BOOK-PRESSES. How then did they bestow their books after they had become too numerous to be kept in the church? The answer to this question is a very curious one, when we consider what our climate is, and indeed what the climate of the whole of Europe is, during the winter months. The centre of the monastic life was the cloister. Brethren were not allowed to congregate in any other part of the conventual buildings, except when they went into the frater, or dining-hall, for their meals, or at certain hours in certain seasons into the warming-house (*calefactorium*). In the cloister accordingly they kept their books; and there they sat and studied, or conducted the schooling of the novices and choir-boys in winter and in summer alike.

Such a locality as this could not have been very favourable to the preservation of the books themselves. They, however, had a certain amount of protection which was denied to their readers, for they were shut up in presses. The word used for these, *armarium*, is the same as that which was applied by the Romans to their bookcases; and probably the idea of such a piece of furniture was due to a far-off echo of ancient usage. The official who had charge of the books did not derive his name from them, as in modern times, but from the presses which contained them—for he was uniformly styled *armarius*.

CARRELLS AND PRESSES AT DURHAM. As time went on, greater comfort was introduced. The windows of the walk of the cloister where the presses stood, usually the walk next the Church, were glazed—and sometimes not merely with white glass, but with mottoes alluding to the authors whose works were near at hand; while in some monasteries the elder monks were provided with small wooden studies, called "carrells." A description of the whole system has been preserved for us in that curious book *The Rites of Durham*; but it must be remembered that this represents the customs of the convent just before the suppression, and therefore gives no idea of the rigour of an earlier time.

Part of the north walk of the cloister, Durham.

In the north syde of the Cloister, from the corner over against the Church dour to the corner over againste the Dorter dour, was all fynely glased from the hight to the sole within a litle of the grownd into the Cloister garth. And in every wyndowe iij Pewes or Carrells, where every one of the old Monks had his carrell, severall by himselfe, that, when they had dyned, they dyd resort to that place of Cloister, and there studyed upon there books, every one in his carrell, all the after nonne, unto evensong tyme. This was there exercise every daie.

BOOK-PRESSES IN WALLS All there pewes or carrells was all fynely wainscotted and verie close, all but the forepart, which had carved wourke that gave light in at ther carrell doures of wainscott. And in every carrell was a deske to lye there bookes on. And the carrells was no greater then from one stanchell of the wyndowe to another.

And over against the carrells against the church wall did stande certaine great almeries [or cupbords] of waynscott all full of bookes [with great store of ancient manuscripts to help them in their study], wherein did lye as well the old auncyent written Doctors of the Church as other prophane authors with dyverse other holie mens wourks, so that every one dyd studye what Doctor pleased them best, havinge the Librarie at all tymes to goe studie in besydes there carrells.

No example of an English monastic book-press has survived, so far as I have been able to discover; but it would be rash to say that none exists. Meanwhile I will shew you a French example of a press, from the sacristy of the Cathedral at Bayeux, but I cannot be sure that it was originally intended to hold books. M. Viollet-Le-Duc, from whom I borrow it, decides that it was probably made early in the thirteenth century.

Cupboard from sacristy of Bayeux Cathedral.

The Durham *Rites* speak only of book-presses standing in the cloister against the walls; but it was not unusual to have recesses *OF CLOISTER AT WORCESTER.* in the wall itself, fitted with shelves, and probably closed by a door. Two such are to be seen at Worcester, immediately to the north of the chapter-house door. Each is about ten feet wide by two feet deep.

Book-recess, east walk of the cloister, Worcester.

A similar receptacle for books seems to have been contemplated in Augustinian Houses, for in the Customs of the Augustinian Priory of Barnwell, written towards the end of the thirteenth century, the following passage occurs:

> The press in which the books are kept ought to be lined inside with wood, that the damp of the walls may not moisten or stain the books. This press should be divided vertically as well as horizontally by sundry partitions, on which the books may be ranged so as to be separated from one another; for fear they be packed so close as to injure each other, or delay those who want them.

Recesses such as these were developed in Cistercian houses into a small square room without a window, and but little larger than *CISTERCIAN PRACTICE.*

an ordinary cupboard. In the plans of Clairvaux and Kirkstall this room is placed between the chapter-house and the transept of the church; and similar rooms, in similar situations, have been found at Fountains, Beaulieu, Tintern, Netley, etc. The catalogue, made 1396, of the Cistercian Abbey at Meaux in Holderness, now totally destroyed, gives us a glimpse of the internal arrangement of one of these rooms. The books were placed on shelves against the walls, and even over the door. Again, the catalogue of the House of White Canons at Titchfield in Hampshire, dated 1400, shews that the books were kept in a small room, on shelves there called *columpnæ*, set against the walls. It is obvious that no study could have gone forward in such places as these; they must have been intended for security only, and to replace the wooden presses used elsewhere.

LIBRARIES IN FIFTEENTH CENTURY. As time went on, the number of the books would naturally increase, and by the beginning of the fifteenth century the larger monasteries at least had accumulated many hundred volumes. For instance, at Christ Church, Canterbury, at the beginning of the 14th century, there were 698. These had to be bestowed in various parts of the House without order or selection,—in presses set up wherever a vacant corner could be found—to the great inconvenience, we may be sure, of the more studious monks, or of scholars who came to consult them. To remedy such a state of things a definite room was constructed for books—in addition to the presses in the cloister, which were still retained for the books in daily use. A few instances of this will suffice. At Christ Church, Canterbury, a library was built between 1414 and 1443 by Archbishop Chichele, over the Prior's Chapel; at Durham between 1416 and 1446 by Prior Wessyngton, over the old sacristy; at Citeaux in 1480, over the writing-room (*scriptorium*); at Clairvaux between 1495 and 1503, in the same position; at S. Victor in Paris—an Augustinian House—between 1501 and 1508; and at S. Germain des Prés in the same city about 1513, over the south cloister.

S. GERMAIN DES PRÉS. Most of us, I take it, have more or less imperfect ideas of the appearance of a great monastery in the days of its completeness; and information on this point is unfortunately much more defective for our own country than it is for France. In illustration, therefore, of what I have been saying about the position of monastic libraries, I will next shew you two bird's-eye views of the Benedictine House of S. Germain des Prés, Paris. The first, dated 1687, shews the library over the south walk of the cloister, where it was placed in 1513. It must not, however, be supposed that no library existed before this. On the contrary, the House seems to have had one from the first foundation, and so early as the thirteenth century it could be consulted by strangers, and books borrowed from it. The second view, dated 1723, shews a still further extension of the library. It has now invaded the west side of the cloister, which has received an upper storey, and even the external appearance of the venerable refectory, which was respected when nearly all the rest of the buildings were rebuilt in a classical style, has been sacrificed to a similar gallery. The united lengths of these three rooms must have been little short of 324 feet. This library was at the disposal of all scholars who desired to use it. When the Revolution came it contained more than 49,000 printed books, and 7000 manuscripts. The fittings belonged to the period of its latest extension: they appear to have been sumptuous, but for my present object, uninteresting.

Views of S. Germain des Prés: (1) from Franklin, "Anciennes Bibliothèques de Paris," i. 126; (2) from Bouillart, "Histoire de l'Abbaye de S. Germain des Préz."

CHRIST CHURCH, CANTERBURY.

At Canterbury the library, built as I have said, over the Prior's Chapel, was 60 feet long, by 22 feet broad; and we know, from some memoranda written in 1508, when a number of books were sent to be bound or repaired, that it contained sixteen bookcases, each of which had four shelves. I have calculated that this library could have contained about 2000 volumes.

CITEAUX.

I have shewn you a Benedictine House, and will next shew you a bird's-eye view of Citeaux, the parent house of the Cistercian Order, founded at the close of the eleventh century. The original was taken, so far as I can make out, about 1500, at any rate before the primitive buildings had been seriously altered. The library here occupied two positions—under the roof between the dormitory and the refectory (which must have been extremely inconvenient); and subsequently it was rebuilt in an isolated situation on the north side of the second cloister, over the writing-room (*scriptorium*). This was also the position of the new library at Clairvaux—the other great Cistercian House in France—the fame of which was equal to, if not greater than, that of Citeaux. Of this latter library we have two descriptions; the first written in 1517, the second in 1723.

CLAIRVAUX.   *View of Citeaux: from Viollet-Le-Duc, "Dictionnaire de l'Architecture,"* i. 271.

The former account, by the secretary of the Queen of Sicily, who visited Clairvaux 13 July 1517, is as follows:

> On the same side of the cloister are fourteen studies, where the monks write and study, and over the said studies is the new library, to which one mounts by a broad and lofty spiral staircase from the aforesaid cloister. This library is 189 feet long, by 17 feet wide. In it are 48 seats (*bancs*), and in each seat 4 shelves (*poulpitres*) furnished with books on all subjects, but chiefly theology; the greater number of the said books are of vellum, and written by hand, richly storied and illuminated. The building that contains the said library is magnificent, built of stone, and excellently lighted on both sides with fine large windows, well glazed, looking out on the said cloister and the burial-ground of the brethren.... The said library is paved throughout with small tiles adorned with various designs.

The description written in 1723, by the learned Benedictines to whom we owe the *Voyage Littéraire*, is equally interesting:

CLAIRVAUX.   From the great cloister you proceed into the cloister of conversation, so called because the brethren are allowed to converse there. In this cloister there are 12 or 15 little cells, all of a row, where the brethren formerly used to write books; for this reason they are still called at the present day the writing-rooms. Over these cells is the Library, the building for which is large, vaulted, well lighted, and stocked with a large number of manuscripts, fastened by chains to desks; but there are not many printed books.

In the great cloister, on the side next the Chapter House, the same observer noted "books chained on wooden desks, which brethren can come and read when they please." The library was for serious study, the cloister for daily reading, probably in the main devotional.

CHRIST'S HOSPITAL. If my time were unlimited I could describe to you several other fifteenth century monastic libraries, but I feel that I must content myself with only one more—that of the Franciscan House in London, commonly called Christ's Hospital. The first stone of this library was laid by Sir Richard Whittington, 21 October, 1421, and by Christmas Day in the following year the roof was finished. Stow tells us that it was 129 feet long by 31 feet broad; and the Letters Patent of Henry the Eighth add that it had 28 desks, and 28 double settles of wainscot. The whole building—so well worth preservation—has been totally destroyed, but I am able to shew you a view of it.

Library of Christ's Hospital: from Trollope's "History of Christ's Hospital," p. 105.

This view is an excellent illustration of the point on which I have insisted, namely, that in the course of the fifteenth century the great religious Houses—no matter to what Order they belonged—found that their books had become too numerous for the localities primitively intended for them, and began to build special libraries—usually over some existing structure; or—in other words—established a library of reference, which was not unfrequently thrown open to scholars in general, who were allowed to borrow books from it, on execution of an indenture, or deposit of a sufficient pledge. "It is safer to fall back on a pledge, than to proceed against an individual," said the Customs of the Priory at Abingdon.

ANALOGY BETWEEN In what way were these monastic libraries fitted up? No trace of any monastic fittings has survived, so far as I am aware, either in England, or in France, or in Italy; and even M. Viollet-Le-Duc dismisses "The Library" in a few brief sentences, of which the keynote is despair. My own view is that a close analogy may be traced between the fittings of monastic libraries and those of collegiate libraries; and that when we understand the one we shall understand the other.

MONASTERIES AND

Libraries in the Medieval and Renaissance Periods

COLLEGES. The collegiate system was in no sense of the word monastic, indeed it was to a certain extent established to counteract monastic influence; but it is absurd to suppose that the younger communities would borrow nothing from the elder—especially when we reflect that the monastic system had completed at least seven centuries of successful existence before Walter de Merton was moved to found a college; that many of the subsequent founders of colleges were churchmen, if not actually monks; and that there were monastic colleges at both Universities. Further, as we have seen that study was specially enjoined upon the monks by S. Benedict, it is precisely in the direction of study that we should expect to find common features in the two sets of communities. And this, in fact, is what came to pass. An examination of the statutes affecting the library in the codes imposed upon the colleges of Oxford and Cambridge shews that their provisions were borrowed directly from the monastic Customs. The resemblances are too striking to be accidental. Take, for instance, this clause, from the statutes of Oriel College, Oxford, dated 1329:

COLLEGE STATUTES. The common books (*communes libri*) of the House are to be brought out and inspected once a year, on the feast of the Commemoration of Souls [2 November], in presence of the Provost or his deputy, and of the Scholars [Fellows].

Every one of them in turn, in order of seniority, may select a single book which either treats of the science to which he is devoting himself, or which he requires for his use. This he may keep until the same festival in the succeeding year, when a similar selection of books is to take place, and so on, from year to year. If there should happen to be more books than persons, those that remain are to be selected in the same manner.

Bishop Bateman—who had been educated in the priory at Norwich, and whose brother was an abbot—gave statutes to Trinity Hall, Cambridge, in 1350, with similar provisions, and the addition that certain books "are to remain continuously in the library-chamber, fastened with iron chains, for the common use of the Fellows." These were copied by Wykeham at New College, Oxford, but with extended provisions for lending books to students, and a direction that all the books "which remain unassigned after the Fellows have made their selection are to be fastened with iron chains, and remain for ever in the common Library." This statute was repeated at King's College, Cambridge, and at several colleges in Oxford.

ANNUAL AUDIT OF BOOKS. Let me now remind you of Archbishop Lanfranc's statute for English Benedictines, dated 1070, which was based, as he himself tells us, on the general monastic practice of his time:

> On the Monday after the first Sunday in Lent, before brethren come into the Chapter House, the librarian (*custos librorum*) shall have had a carpet laid down, and all the books got together upon it, except those which a year previously had been assigned for reading. These brethren are to bring with them, when they come into the Chapter House, each his book in his hand....
>
> Then the librarian shall read a statement as to the manner in which brethren have had books during the past year. As each brother hears his name pronounced he is to give back the book which had been entrusted to him for reading; and he whose conscience accuses him of not having read the book through which he had received, is to fall on his face, confess his fault, and entreat forgiveness.
>
> The librarian shall then make a fresh distribution of books, namely, a different volume to each brother for his reading.

EARLIEST BOOK-DESK. You will agree with me, I feel sure, that this statute, or similar provisions extracted from other regulations, is the source of the collegiate provisions for an annual audit and distribution of books; while the reservation of the undistributed volumes, and their chaining for common use in a library, was in accordance with the unwritten practice of the monasteries. This being the case I think that we are justified in assuming that the internal fittings of the libraries would be identical also; and it must be further remembered that both collegiate and monastic libraries were being fitted up during the same period, the fifteenth century.

EARLIEST BOOK-DESK. When books were first placed in a separate room, fastened with iron chains, for the use of the Fellows of a college or the monks of a convent, the piece of furniture used was, I take it, an elongated lectern or desk, of a convenient height for a seated reader to use. The books lay on their sides on the desk, and were attached by chains to a horizontal bar above it. There were at least two libraries in this University fitted with such desks, at the colleges of Pembroke and Queens'; and that it was a common form abroad is proved by its appearance in a French translation of the first book of the *Consolations of Philosophy* of Boethius, which I lately found in the British Museum[1], executed towards the end of the fifteenth century (fig. 1).

BOOK-DESKS AT
ZUTPHEN.

Fig. 1. Interior of a library: from a MS. of a French translation of the first book of the Consolations of Philosophy of Boethius.

---

[1] MSS. Harl. 4335.

One example at least of these fittings still exists, in the library attached to the church of S. Wallberg, at Zutphen in Holland. This library was built in its present position in 1555, but I suspect that some of the fittings, those namely which are more richly ornamented, were removed from an earlier library. Each of these desks is 9 feet long by 5 feet 6 inches high; and, as you will see directly, a man can sit and read at them very conveniently. I shall shew you first a general view of part of the library (fig. 2); and, secondly, a single desk (fig. 3).

Such cases as these must have been in use at the Sorbonne, where a library was first established in 1289 for books chained for the common convenience of the Fellows (*in communem sociorum utilitatem*). A description of this library, based probably on records now lost, has been given by Claude Héméré (Librarian 1638-1643) in his MS. history. This I proceed to translate:

LIBRARY OF THE SORBONNE.

Fig. 3. Desk in the library at Zutphen: from a photograph.

The old library was contained under one roof. It was firmly and solidly built, and was 120 feet long by 36 feet

Libraries in the Medieval and Renaissance Periods

broad. Further, that it might be the more safe from the danger of being burnt, should any house in the neighbourhood catch fire, there was a sufficient interval between it and every dwelling-house. Each side was pierced with 19 windows of equal size, that plenty of daylight both from the east and the west (for this was the direction of the room) might fall upon the desks, and fill the whole length and breadth of the library. There were 28 desks, marked with the letters of the alphabet, five feet high, and so arranged that they were separated by a moderate interval. They were loaded with books, all of which were chained, that no sacrilegious hand might [carry them off. These chains were attached to the right-hand board of every book] so that they might be readily thrown aside, and reading not be interfered with. Moreover the volumes could be opened and shut without difficulty. A reader who sat down in the space between two desks, as they rose to a height of five feet as I said above, neither saw nor disturbed any one else who might be reading or writing in another place by talking or by any other interruption, unless the other student wished it, or paid attention to any question that might be put to him. It was required, by the ancient rules of the library, that reading, writing, and handling of books should go forward in complete silence.

LIBRARY OF THE SORBONNE. This system must have been very wasteful as regards space; for only a few volumes, say a couple of dozen, could be accommodated on a single desk. As books accumulated therefore some other form of case had to be devised, which would accommodate more volumes than could be consulted at once. The desk could not be dispensed with so long as books were chained, but one or more shelves were added to it. This addition was effected in two ways, according as the books were to stand on their ends, or to lie on their sides.

MERTON COLLEGE, OXFORD. As an illustration of the former plan I will take the library of Merton College, Oxford, attributed by tradition to William Reade, Bishop of Chichester 1368-85; and it has been so little altered that it may be taken as a type of a medieval collegiate or monastic library. It is a long narrow room, as all medieval libraries were, with equidistant windows, and the bookcases stand at right angles to the walls in the spaces between each pair of windows, in front of which is the seat for the reader. Each bookcase had originally two shelves only above the desk. I will shew you, first, a general view of the interior of this library, and then a single bookcase and seat.

Merton College, Oxford: (1) general view of the interior of the Library; (2) a single bookcase as at present.

CHAINING OF BOOKS.

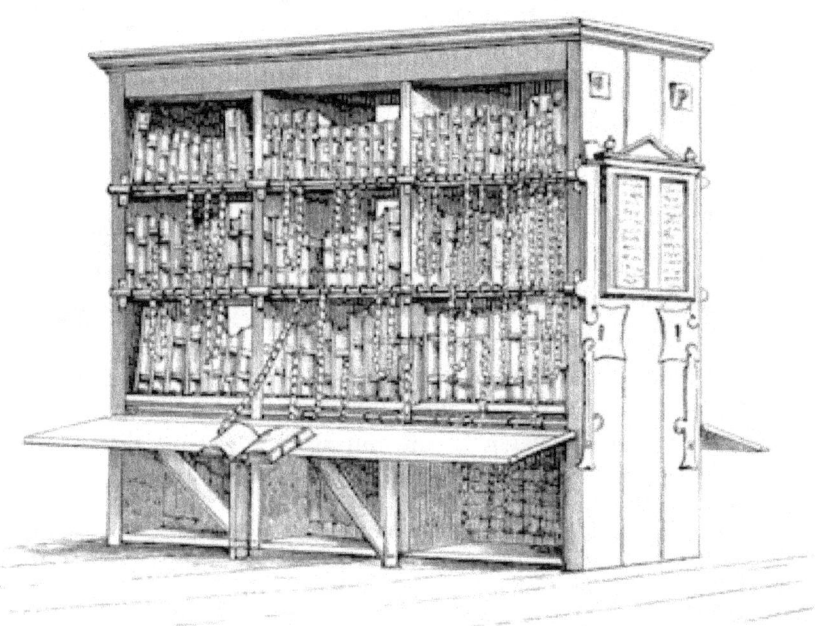

Fig. 4. Bookcase in Hereford Cathedral. (Lent by the Syndics of the University Press.)

Having said thus much about chaining, I return to the Merton The system of chaining, as adopted in this country, would allow of the books being readily taken down from the shelves, and laid on the desk for reading. One end of the chain was attached to the middle of the upper edge of the right-hand board; the other to a ring which played on a bar set in front of the shelf on which the book stood. The fore-edge of the books, not the back, was turned forwards. A swivel, usually in the middle of the chain, prevented tangling. The chains varied in length according to the distance of the shelf from the desk. The bar was kept in place by a rather elaborate system of iron-work attached to the end of the bookcase, and secured by a lock which often required two keys—that is, the presence of two officials—to open it. To illustrate this I will shew you a sketch of one of the bookcases in Hereford Cathedral (fig. 4).

CHAINING OF BOOKS. bookcases. Cases similar to these were evidently in use in the library of Christ Church, Canterbury, where the memoranda I mentioned record four shelves—that is, two on each side—in each bookcase, and also at Clairvaux, where a similar feature was observed. The design was evidently much admired, for we find cases on a similar plan, but larger, elsewhere in Oxford, as at the Colleges of Corpus Christi, S. John's, Trinity, Jesus, and in the Bodleian Library.

TRINITY HALL, CAMBRIDGE. *Bookcase in the Library of Corpus Christi College, Oxford.*

Another device for combining desk with shelf is to be seen at Trinity Hall, Cambridge, and, as these cases were set up after 1626, we have here a curious instance of a deliberate return to ancient forms. There is evidence that there once existed below the shelf a second desk, which could be drawn in and out as required, so that a reader could stand or sit as he pleased, as you will see from the next illustration.

Bookcase in the Library of Trinity Hall, Cambridge.

UNIVERSITY OF LEIDEN. The University of Leiden in Holland adopted a modification of this design, for there the shelf is above the desk, and readers could only stand to use the books (fig. 5).

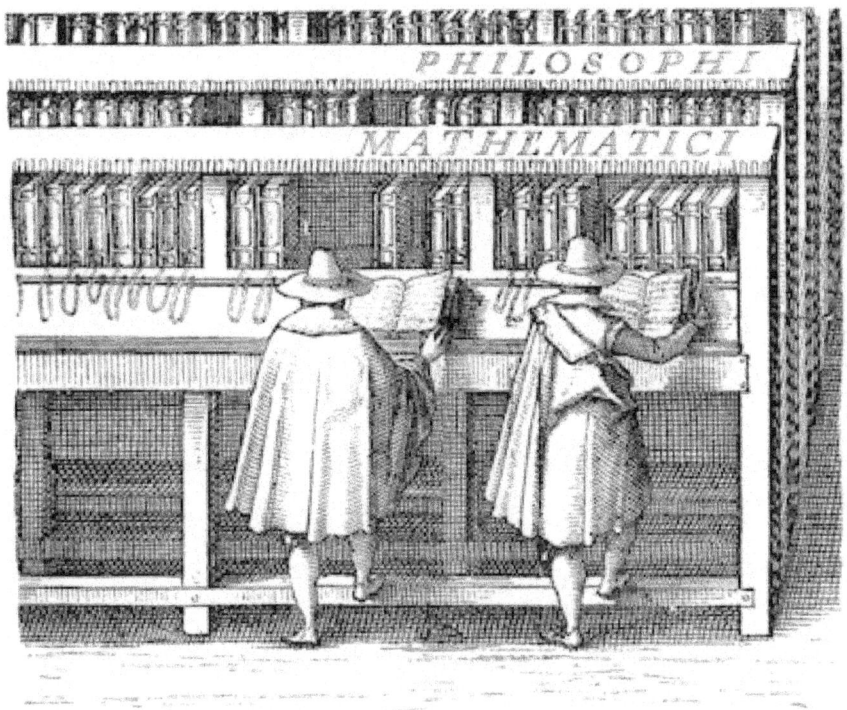

Fig. 5. Bookcases in the library of the University of Leiden: from a print by J.C. Woudanus, dated 1610. (Lent by the Syndics of the University Press.)

An arrangement analogous to this was adopted at Citeaux, as we may gather from the catalogue, drawn up in 1480. I will not trouble you with details, but merely say that there was evidently a shelf below the desk as well as one above it. The cases therefore resembled those at Leiden, with this difference; and they were also probably of such a height that a reader could conveniently sit at them.

LIBRARY AT CESENA.

On the continent, where elaborate bindings came early into fashion, sometimes protected by equally elaborate bosses at their corners, it would have been impossible to arrange the volumes as we did side by side on the shelves. It therefore became the fashion to place a shelf below the desk, and to lay the books upon it on their sides. The earliest library fitted in this manner that I have been able to discover is at Cesena in North Italy. It was built in 1452, by Domenico Malatesta Novello, for the convent of S. Francesco. It is possible,

Libraries in the Medieval and Renaissance Periods

therefore, that the parent house of S. Francesco at Assisi, which had a large library, divided, so early as 1381, into a *Libreria publica* and a *Libreria secreta*, had similar bookcases. I am going to shew you a general view of the room, which has a thoroughly medieval character, next the cases (fig. 6), and thirdly a single book with its chain (fig. 7). You will observe that the seats for the reader are no longer independent, but are combined with the bookcase.

*LIBRARY AT
CESENA.*

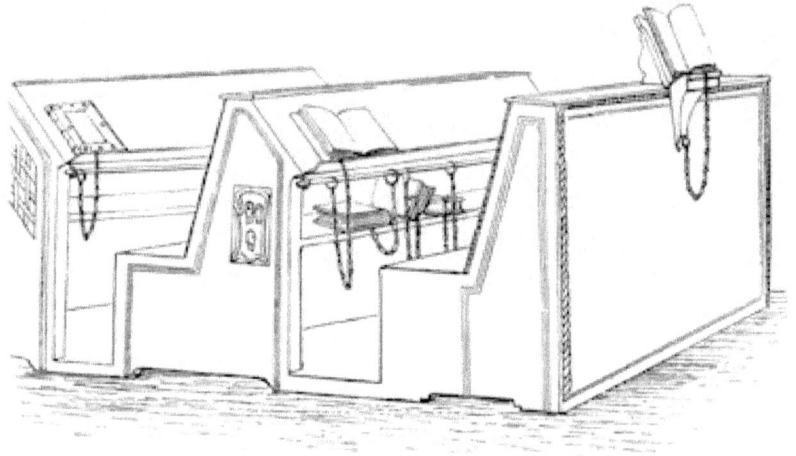

Fig. 6. Bookcases at west end of south side of Library, Cesena.

These cases no doubt suggested those in the Medicean library at Florence, begun in 1525 by Michael Angelo. The cases, perhaps the finest specimens in existence of wood-carving as applied to this style of work, were designed by other artists shortly after the completion of the room.

LIBRARY AT CESENA.

Fig. 7. Part of a single bookcase in the Library, Cesena.

Libraries in the Medieval and Renaissance Periods

S. JOHN'S COLLEGE.

Bookcase in the Medicean Library at Florence.

In English libraries at least bookcases arranged on what I may term the Oxford type were in general use throughout the sixteenth and seventeenth centuries. The invention of printing had largely increased the number of volumes, and at the same time diminished their value, so that chaining was no longer necessary. When it had been abandoned neither a desk, nor a seat in close proximity to the books, was required. In consequence, though libraries continued to be built on the ancient type with numerous windows close to the floor, it was possible to alter the old cases, or to make new ones, with a far larger number of shelves than heretofore; and when further space for books was needed, low cases were interposed between each pair of tall ones. A splendid specimen of this treatment is to be seen at S. John's College, Cambridge, where the bookcases were put up soon after the completion of the library in 1628. Though the plinth and central pilaster have been taken away, and the levels of the shelves changed, their original appearance can be recovered at a glance. On the top of all the low cases there was a desk, in memory of that of ancient times. At the end of the taller cases is a panel to contain the catalogue, here closed by a small door.

Bookcases in S. John's College Library.

Sometimes, as we see at Peterhouse, ancient usage asserted itself so far that a seat was contrived by making the plinth of the tall case project to a sufficient distance. These bookcases were set up between 1641 and 1648.

PETERHOUSE.

Bookcase in Peterhouse Library.

When the necessity for still further space for books became imperative, the seat was given up, or was dropped to the height of a step, as in the bookcases in the south room of the University Library, Cambridge, put up soon after 1649. The carved wing, however, which had masked the ends of it, was retained as an ornament, both there and in the old library at Pembroke College, Cambridge, furnished soon after 1690.

THE ESCURIAL.

Meanwhile a new system of arranging bookcases had come into use on the continent. So far as I have been able to discover, the first library arranged in the way with which we are familiar, namely, with the bookcases set against the walls instead of at right angles to them, is that of the Escurial. These cases were made by Herrera, the architect of the building, in 1584. There is no indication of chaining, but, in conformity with ancient usage, the fore edge of the books, instead of their backs, is turned outwards, and the desk is represented by a shelf, carried all round the room at a convenient height. No doubt so important a structure as this, erected by so mighty a potentate as the King of Spain, would be much talked about, and provoke imitators. Among these, I feel sure, was Cardinal Mazarin, whose library was fitted up in Paris in or about 1647, as a library to be used daily by the public. After his death his books and bookcases were moved to the building in which they may still be seen. I will now shew you views of the two libraries, and you shall decide whether it is not obvious that the one was suggested by the other.

Interior of the Library of the Escurial and of the Bibliothèque Mazarine, Paris.

BIBLIOTHÈQUE MAZARINE.

The new system was not accepted hastily. I believe that Sir Christopher Wren, when he built Trinity College Library in 1695, was the first English architect who ventured to build a library with windows which, as he says himself, "rise high, and give place for the deskes against the walls." I suspect that he borrowed this latter idea from France, which he visited in 1665, and most likely from the Bibliothèque Mazarine, for he has himself recorded his admiration for "the masculine furniture of the Palais Mazarin," though he does not specially mention the library. But he did not discard the ancient arrangement altogether. On the contrary he utilised it so far as to subdivide the room, and provide recesses for the convenience of students. He says:

The disposition of the shelves both along the walls and breaking out from the walls must needes prove very convenient and gracefull, and the best way for the students will be to have a litle square table in each celle with 2 chaires. The necessity of bringing windowes and dores to answer to the old building leaves two squarer places at the endes, and 4

TRINITY COLLEGE LIBRARY.

Libraries in the Medieval and Renaissance Periods

lesser celles not to study in, but to be shut up with some neat lattice dores for archives.

One compartment of Trinity College Library.

I need hardly say that neither this library, nor any of those built by Wren's pupils or imitators, shew traces of chaining. The old fashion, however, lingered. In 1651 Humphrey Cheetham directed the books he gave to certain specified parish-churches near Manchester to be chained; in 1694 James Leaver gave books to the grammar-school at Bolton in Lancashire which were chained in a cupboard very like the *armarium* of a monastic cloister;

PRIVATE LIBRARIES.

Book-cupboard and desk at Bolton, Lancashire. The former is lettered: "The gift of Mr James Leaver, citison of London 1694."

and at All Saints Church, Hereford, a collection of books bequeathed in 1715 was chained to ordinary shelves set against the walls, as may still be seen. This very obvious way of disposing of books evidently shocked old-fashioned people, for Cole the antiquary, writing in 1703, could still speak of the arrangement of shelves against the walls as *à la moderne*.

The libraries I have been describing were more or less public, and I should like, before I conclude, to shew you how books were bestowed in the studies of individual scholars—whether royal, monastic, or secular.

ISIDORE, BISHOP OF SEVILLE.

I conceive that for many centuries after the beginning of the Christian era the methods of the ancient world were followed; and that private libraries were arranged upon the Roman model in presses, with busts, mottoes, and the like. Such was the library of Isidore, Bishop of Seville (601-636). He was a voluminous writer, and seems to have had a voluminous library, divided, if I interpret the arrangements correctly, among fourteen presses, each ornamented by one or more portrait-busts or medallions with suitable verses beneath them. The series concludes with a notice *Ad interventorem*, a person whom we may call *A talkative intruder*:

Non patitur quenquam coram se scriba loquentem:
Non est hic quod agas, garrule, perge foras.

How useful such an admonition would be in modern libraries, if only it could be enforced!

So late as the end of the twelfth century I find a Bishop who bequeathed his library to a church describing it as "the contents of my press (*plenarium armarium meum*)."

Gradually, however, other methods came into fashion, due probably to the introduction of the handsome bindings of which I have already spoken. Some particulars have fortunately been preserved of the cost of fitting up a certain tower in the Louvre between 1364 and 1368, to contain the books belonging to Charles the Fifth of France, from which much useful information may be extracted. The fittings of the older library in the palace on the Isle de la Cité were to be taken down and altered, and set up in the new room. Two carpenters are paid for "having taken to pieces all the cases (*bancs*) and two wheels (*roes*), that is revolving desks, which were in the king's library in the palace, and transported them to the Louvre...; and for having put all together again, and hung up the cases (*lettrins*) in the two upper stages of the tower that looks toward the Falconry, to put the king's books in; and for having panelled ... the first of those two stories all round inside." Next a wire-worker (*cagetier*) is paid "for having made trellises of wire in front of two casements and two windows ... to keep out birds and other beasts (*oyseaux et autres bestes*) by reason of, and protection for, the books that shall be placed there."

LIBRARY-TOWER IN THE LOUVRE.

The words *bancs* and *lettrins*, which I have translated "cases," are both frequently used. The first commonly denotes the cases in monastic libraries, and the second is the usual word for a reading-desk. I think, therefore, that the two words were applied to describe the same piece of furniture, as "stall" and "desk" were with us. I am now going to shew you two pictures of rooms arranged for study, which fit the above description very well. The first is from a French translation of Boccaccio, *Des cas des maleureux nobles hommes et femmes*, written and illuminated in Flanders for King Henry the Seventh[1]. Two gentlemen are studying at a revolving desk, which can be raised or

LIBRARY-TOWER IN THE LOUVRE.

---

[1] MSS. Mus. Brit. 14. E. V.

lowered by a screw. This is evidently the "wheel" of the French king's library. Behind are their books, either resting on a desk hung against the wall (which is panelled), or lying on a shelf beneath the desk. The second is also Flemish, of the same date, from a copy of the *Miroir historial*[1]. It represents a monk, probably the author of the book, writing in his study. Behind him are three desks, one above the other, hung against the wall, with books, as in the first picture, resting upon them.

DESKS HUNG TO THE WALLS. Some such arrangement as this must have been long in fashion. Libraries such as those of Diane de Poitiers and Francis the First could not have been bestowed in any other way; and in fact, when books are enriched with metal-work, or have specially elaborate ornaments on their sides, a desk of some sort is indispensable.

DESK AND CUPBOARD. Humbler scholars had to content themselves with small cupboards constructed in the thickness of the wall, or hung against it, as in the picture I will next shew you, from a French translation of Valerius Maximus, copied for King Edward the Fourth, and dated 1479[2]. You will observe that the lower part of the window is fitted with trellises as in the French king's library, not casements. The upper part only is glazed.

Another, and apparently very usual way of bestowing books, especially when they were not numerous, was to place them in a sort of cupboard under the sloping desk on which the owner read or wrote. An excellent specimen of this device—which Richard de Bury specially commends, as being modelled on the Ark, in the side of which the book of the Law was put—is to be found in the *Ship of Fools* (1498). Another, of a curiously modern type, occurs in an *Hours* in the Fitzwilliam Museum, Cambridge, executed about 1445 for Isabel, Duchess of Brittany.

CONCLUSION. Sometimes this book-cupboard supported a revolving desk, which could be raised or depressed by the help of a central screw—like those I shewed you just now; sometimes the desk alone appears, with books laid on it. The

---

[1] MSS. Mus. Brit. 14. E. I.
[2] MSS. Mus. Brit. 18. E. IV.

forms given to these pieces of furniture by the ingenuity of those who made them are infinite; and they often include beautiful designs for armchairs, fitted with desks for writing. I will shew you just one—not because it is specially beautiful, but because it gives a quaint picture of a scholar's room at the beginning of the fifteenth century[1].

CONCLUSION.

Here Time—as represented by yonder clock—holds up his finger and bids me stop. I would fain have shewn you more pictures—but I hope that you have seen a sufficient number to give you some idea of the surroundings in which our forefathers read and wrote. I am sure that only in this way can we realise that they were real living people—not mere names. Their modes of thought were far different from ours; they may have wasted their time in verbal subtleties, and uncritical tales; but the more we study what they did, the more we shall realise how laborious, how artistic, how conscientious they were; and amid all the developments of the nineteenth century, we shall gratefully confess that the Middle Ages rocked the cradle of our knowledge, and that we "See but their hope become reality."

---

[1] MSS. Mus. Brit. 20. B. XX.

Also from Benediction Books …
The Care of Books
An Essay on the Development of Libraries and their Fittings , from the earliest times to the end of the Eighteenth Century.
John Willis Clark M.A., F.S.A.
Benediction Classics, Oxford, 2011
436 pages
978-1-78139-033-7

Available from www.amazon.com, www.amazon.co.uk

The Care of Books is an engaging text, considering not only the preservation of books, but also their physical ordering. Clark draws on archival and archaeological sources, displaying his wide range of interests. Clark writes in the Preface that 'The subject was entirely new' and all the illustrations were purchased, commissioned or photographed by him for the 1901 publication.

This edition comes with over 150 illustrations, over 500 footnotes and the original index.

**The Middle Parts of Fortune:
Somme and Ancre, 1916**
Frederic Manning
Benediction Classics, 2011
260 pages
ISBN: 978-1-84902-466-2

Available from www.amazon.com,
www.amazon.co.uk

First published in 1929, it is now available as a brand new book. The story is an account of the lives of ordinary soldiers. The central character, Bourne is an enigmatic character and Manning tells his own wartime experiences through him. It is forcibly written, too forcibly for the sensibilities of the time, and a censored version was produced in 1930 under the title 'Her Privates We'.

The Gracchi Marius and Sulla Epochs Of Ancient History - with original maps and sidenotes as sub headings
A. H. Beesley
Benediction Classics, 2011
178 pages
ISBN: 978-1-84902-417-4

Available from www.amazon.com,
www.amazon.co.uk

Epochs of ancient history, the Gracchi, Marius and Sulla was written by A.H. Beesley in 1921. It is a historical text, describing a time of crisis in the Roman Empire, which eventually culminated in its demise. Beesley sought to provide the most a consistent and faithful account of the leaders and legislation of this era. He drew on Long's 'History of the Decline of the Roman Republic' and Mommsen's 'History of Rome'. This edition comes complete with the original maps and the sidenotes have been converted into subheadings.

Also from Benediction Books …
Wandering Between Two Worlds: Essays on Faith and Art
Anita Mathias
Benediction Books, 2007
152 pages
ISBN: 0955373700

Available from www.amazon.com, www.amazon.co.uk

In these wide-ranging lyrical essays, Anita Mathias writes, in lush, lovely prose, of her naughty Catholic childhood in Jamshedpur, India; her large, eccentric family in Mangalore, a sea-coast town converted by the Portuguese in the sixteenth century; her rebellion and atheism as a teenager in her Himalayan boarding school, run by German missionary nuns, St. Mary's Convent, Nainital; and her abrupt religious conversion after which she entered Mother Teresa's convent in Calcutta as a novice. Later rich, elegant essays explore the dualities of her life as a writer, mother, and Christian in the United States-- Domesticity and Art, Writing and Prayer, and the experience of being "an alien and stranger" as an immigrant in America, sensing the need for roots.

About the Author

Anita Mathias is the author of *Wandering Between Two Worlds: Essays on Faith and Art*. She has a B.A. and M.A. in English from Somerville College, Oxford University, and an M.A. in Creative Writing from the Ohio State University, USA. Anita won a National Endowment of the Arts fellowship in Creative Nonfiction in 1997. She lives in Oxford, England with her husband, Roy, and her daughters, Zoe and Irene.

Anita's website:
    http://www.anitamathias.com, and
Anita's blog Dreaming Beneath the Spires:
    http://dreamingbeneaththespires.blogspot.com

The Church That Had Too Much
Anita Mathias
Benediction Books, 2010
52 pages
ISBN: 9781849026567

Available from www.amazon.com, www.amazon.co.uk

The Church That Had Too Much was very well-intentioned. She wanted to love God, she wanted to love people, but she was both hampered by her muchness and the abundance of her possessions, and beset by ambition, power struggles and snobbery. Read about the surprising way The Church That Had Too Much began to resolve her problems in this deceptively simple and enchanting fable.

About the Author

Anita Mathias is the author of *Wandering Between Two Worlds: Essays on Faith and Art*. She has a B.A. and M.A. in English from Somerville College, Oxford University, and an M.A. in Creative Writing from the Ohio State University, USA. Anita won a National Endowment of the Arts fellowship in Creative Nonfiction in 1997. She lives in Oxford, England with her husband, Roy, and her daughters, Zoe and Irene.

Anita's website:
    http://www.anitamathias.com, and
Anita's blog Dreaming Beneath the Spires:
    http://dreamingbeneaththespires.blogspot.com

www.ingramcontent.com/pod-product-compliance
Lightning Source LLC
LaVergne TN
LVHW041205250326
834689LV00001BA/13